Look, Pat and Nan!

by Julia Nash
illustrated by Patrick Chapin

Scott Foresman

Editorial Offices: Glenview, Illinois • New York, New York
Sales Offices: Reading, Massachusetts • Duluth, Georgia
Glenview, Illinois • Carrollton, Texas • Menlo Park, California

Look at the  cow and the can!